J(

DYING, I

To the patients and staff,
past and present, living and dead,
with whom I worked.

JOHN QUINLAN

Journey through dying death and bereavement

THE COLUMBA PRESS
DUBLIN 1989

First edition, 1989, published by
THE COLUMBA PRESS
93 The Rise, Mount Merrion,
Blackrock, Co Dublin, Ireland.

Origination by The Columba Press
Printed in Ireland by
Genprint Ltd, Dublin.

ISBN: 0 948183 71 3

Imprimatur:
+ Diarmaid Ó Súilleabháin
Bishop of Kerry
April 17th 1989

Contents

Preface

My experiences, especially as a hospital chaplain and also as a curate, caused me to reflect on dying, death and grief. I needed to put these experiences in perspective in my own life if I was to attempt to minister to people who were sick, dying or bereaved. This book is based on my experiences as a chaplain to Tralee General Hospital, Tralee, Co Kerry; the former St Catherine's Hospital, Tralee, Co. Kerry; as a trainee chaplain at St Joseph's Medical Center, South Bend, Indiana, USA, Willmar Regional Treatment Centre, Willmar, Minnesota, USA, and Cork Regional Hospital, Cork; and as curate in the Parish of St John the Baptist, Tralee.

The book falls into three parts. Part I, on dying and death, tries to capture some of the anxieties, fears and hopes of those who are seriously ill and/or dying. It includes the story of Tom, who develops a serious illness. We sense his struggle and that of Helen, his wife, and their children as they attempt to cope with Tom's illness. Tom suffered much anguish and felt many hopes before finally accepting death, a death which was not the end but the beginning of a new life with God.

Part II, on bereavement, contains some letters written by Helen after Tom's death. They are an attempt to capture some of the feelings and trauma of bereavement. Bereavement is the complex of emotions we feel after the death of someone we love.

Part III considers Stillbirth and Neo-Natal

Death. It includes the story of a couple who lost their second child by stillbirth. Again it is an attempt to capture some of the anguish of the event. Chapter 8 outlines a suggested hospital policy for the management of stillbirth and neo-natal death. Chapter 9 considers Baptism in relation to Stillbirth, Miscarriage and Neo-Natal Death. In reading this book, one must be conscious of the many things which are communicated only non-verbally in any relationship. These are the things which have to be felt and experienced and cannot be translated in to the written word.

I would like to express sincere gratitude to the following: to God who has given me so much through other people and in life's experiences; to my family and personal friends for their friendship, trust and support; to the patients and relatives, past and present, living and dead, who trusted me with their intimate concerns; to the staff of the different disciplines who cared for them and continually help me with their friendship, support and assistance – they are true pastoral carers; to my Clinical Pastoral Education supervisors in Cork Regional Hospital, Cork, Ireland, St Joseph's Medical Center, South Bend, Indiana, USA, and Willmar Regional Treatment Center, Willmar, Minnesota, USA, who helped me learn about myself and assisted my attempts to learn and develop pastoral skills; to my superiors and fellow priests who encouraged me in my ministry; to the typist who typed and proofread the manuscript.
If this work helps or encourages anyone to get closer to someone who is sick or dying it will have been worthwhile.

John Quinlan

PART I

Dying and Death

CHAPTER ONE

Dying: The Journey

The Background

You may have heard the story of the horse who comes to dinner. At the dining room table everybody sees him, everybody knows he is there, yet everybody ignores him. The guests say nothing hoping that the host doesn't see him. The host says nothing hoping that the guests don't see him. Everybody goes on talking about everything and anything except what is the most obvious – the presence of the horse.

The horse is death, dying or terminal illness. Dying is 'the period of time which more immediately precedes death and in which the person is aware that he/she will soon die'. It varies in length depending on whether it comes quickly from an acute illness or more slowly from a chronic illness, malignant disease, or old age. The exception is sudden death.

In 1965 four theology students of the Chicago Theological Seminary asked a young Swiss psychiatrist, Dr Elizabeth Kübler-Ross to help them with their research project entitled, 'Death as the biggest crisis people face in their lifetime'. Together they decided that the only way to learn about the final stages of life with all its anxieties, fears and hopes was to let the dying patients themselves be their teachers. Only from them could they learn how people respond to this great crisis in life; only in this way could they learn the needs of those preparing for death.

They interviewed hundreds of terminally ill

patients. As a result Dr Kübler-Ross identified and charted a series of psychological and emotional responses through which people prepare for death. They are described in her book *On Death and Dying*. They are identified as:

(i) Shock/Denial/Isolation
(ii) Anger
(iii) Bargaining
(iv) Depression
(v) Acceptance

She noted that *hope* was present right through.

She also noted that:

(i) Most patients were aware of the seriousness of their illness whether they were told or not. Some were told; with others it dawned on them early on; others learned implicitly from the attitudes and behaviour of those around them – hospital staff or whoever: some just knew that they were not well.

(ii) People do not necessarily move through these experiences in chronological order. They move to and fro; some may be present together; some may be skipped; some people never accept.

The Journey

Helen and Tom O'Shea lived in their two-storey semi-detached house in the outskirts of a large town in the midlands. Tom was forty-five and the owner of a small drapery shop in the town. Helen was two years younger. At this time their four children were all school-going. Tomás was attending the local secondary school and studying for his Leaving Certificate. His sister, Mary, was in her second year at the same school. Sheila and Seán were in fifth and second class respectively in the local primary school. In the early weeks of the year Tom felt unwell. Eventually, after some persuasion, he went to see Dr O'Sullivan, his family doctor. Dr O'Sullivan referred him to the hospital for tests. Mr Curtin at the hospital was a serious man. Though he said little, Tom trusted him from the beginning. For Tom those few days in hospital, as he waited for the results of his tests, seemed like a month. Despite various empty reassurances from visitors, his anxiety increased with every passing day. Then one day Mr Curtin told him gently that he had some malignant cells in his bowel. He would, with Tom's consent, operate and do everything he could for him. And he was quite hopeful. Tom was stunned, in fact speechless, for a few hours. Then he wondered, 'maybe it isn't true; Mr Curtin may be wrong; the results may have got mixed up. At least there must be some mistake, whatever it is.' Both Tom and Helen found it difficult to grasp that this just might be a serious illness. He told his brother, Mike, that his illness was'minor' and the operation only precautionary. Helen likewise convinced herself of this and told the children so. Neither of them wanted to see the contradictions. Yet deep down they knew that this was a big operation. And they were afraid. Tom got close to this when he spoke with Joe, his close friend. Joe always had time to listen. He heard Tom's fears and hopes. He didn't deny the possible reality or force it on him.

Tom's operation was scheduled for the following Tuesday morning. Again the waiting seemed endless. At times he wondered if he would wake up after it. At times he felt great hope also. It would be over at mid-day on Tuesday and he would recover in his own time. Mr Curtin and his assistant, Dr Slattery, explained the operation and answered all Tom's questions. When he asked about pain and soreness they assured him that these would be kept under control. Father Pat, the hospital chaplain, visited also. All the staff were very kind. For Tom it was all very strange. He was very lonely, especially on Monday night when Helen and the children said good-bye and wished him well. They cried as they parted.

Tom slept little that night as he waited anxiously for the morning to come. It was a strange sensation to be wheeled into the operating theatre with butter-flies in his stomach and a lump in his throat. The staff reassured him. Mr Curtin and his assistants were there before him. His next memory is waking up in his room.

The days went by and Tom was recovering after his operation. He began to question, 'Why? Why me? – forty-five years old and with Helen and four children – living a simple ordinary life. The children have to be educated. I was always good – never missed Mass, never cheated anyone. Poor old Stephen a few doors away is eighty-five and crippled and seems to be only wanting and waiting to die'. Tom was in an angry mood when Joe visited him at the hospital:

Joe: How are you, Tom?

Tom: I feel terrible. The nurses hurt me. I wouldn't treat anyone like this, not even a dog. They don't seem to realise I had a big operation a few days ago.

Joe: Gosh, you are very cross with some of the nurses, Tom. You say they hurt you.

Tom: They don't understand. I think I'll ring

Helen to come and take me out of here. (*short pause*) The bloody doctor hardly ever shows up. See this thing, (*pointing to drip*) it's bleeding now, but they won't fix it – they'll fool around until it's time to go and leave it to the next shift. The morning shift is very bad. They put this tube in me. I don't need any tube – never had one in my life. They are just too lazy to take me to the toilet.

Joe's patient listening helped Tom to vent his anger.

To add fuel to fire a few days later, Tom developed a complication: his kidneys failed. Confronted with a situation beyond his control, he was very angry and demanding. When someone straightened his pillows he wanted to be left alone. When he was left alone, he called for someone to straighten his pillows. Resenting his family and how active they were, he blamed them for not visiting often enough. He told the nursing staff that they stayed too long. He was angry at God who allowed all this to happen.

Father Pat visited him:

Fr Pat: Hello Tom, how are you this evening?

Tom: Oh I'm all – I don't know – all upset this evening. The visitors upset me ... It's just all wrong. Why did this god-damn thing have to happen to me? Why? Why? On top of everything else at that? They just keep saying the same thing – wait, wait, wait, just two weeks now, just two weeks now. What am I supposed to do – look up at the ceiling for two weeks? They tell me that when I urinate, then I'll know I am O.K., but when, when, when?

Fr Pat:	I know you must feel very angry, Tom. This kidney thing is an added burden. And two weeks sounds like an eternity.
Tom:	Yeh, and they just treat me like a child – do this, do that, wait. What am I going to do? I have to do something about this.
Fr Pat:	It's hard not to be able to do things for yourself.
Tom:	Yes. I mean why me? I come in for my operation and hear nothing about anything else. I don't know nothing about kidneys or anything else. I mean if I come in here for a broken nose, I expect to get it fixed and that's that.
Fr Pat:	You have reason to be angry, Tom. The complications were unexpected.
Tom:	I am angry. I am. What am I supposed to do? I must do something. Am I to wait here till I piss up in the air or what? Listen, come to see me tomorrow. At least I can unburden myself to you and that helps. Come to see me again.
Fr Pat:	Sure, I will, Tom. I'll be round about two o'clock tomorrow. Good-bye for now.
Tom:	Good-bye, Father. See you tomorrow.

Tom appreciated his visitors. They helped him unburden himself. They gave of their time and tolerated his anger. They did not take it personally, make any judgements or argue. He knew that Joe and Father Pat cared and would not abandon him.

At another time, some weeks later, Tom tried to bargain with God. He wanted to postpone the dreaded day. He prayed to be well until Tomás could take over his business – maybe also until Seán made his Confirmation. If this happened he would not ask for anymore. This is his secret though. He told no one except for a confidential mention to Father Pat, who helped simply by joining in the bargaining.

At different times Tom and Helen felt very afraid. Before the operation he feared the anaesthetic: 'Will I wake up again?' He feared that pain and soreness would follow the operation. Sometimes he was afraid that Helen or the children might not accept his illness or appreciate his deeper feelings. What would it be like if he were dependent; if he couldn't support his wife and family; if Helen had to return to work?.

However, Tom received love and support from his family, his friends, his doctors, nurses, priest and carers at home and at the hospital. This and their reassurance that they would always be with him lessened many of his fears. Somehow even before a word was spoken, Tom sensed their caring attitude and knew that they would be with him.

When his kidneys failed, Tom wondered if he would ever get better. He experienced the deep fear of not knowing what next. Lack of information about his condition and its implications disturbed him. Thankfully his doctor explained what he needed to know and in a way that he understood. Mr Curtin understood Tom's need and answered his questions simply and as he required.

Tom went home and after some weeks went back to work in his shop. Some months later he had to return to the hospital. He was weaker and thinner now. Deep within himself he felt a sense of great loss. Neither he nor Helen denied the seriousness of the illness now. Tom was sorrowful that he could not work anymore. He talked endlessly about the things he did that he could no longer do and about the things he was sorry he didn't do. He was comforted when someone remembered and praised his achievements. Likewise Helen was consoled when someone noticed and understood how she felt. The children appreciated the friends who treated them the same as everybody else, yet were sensitive to their sad predicament.

One evening, Claire, one of the nurses, sat by Tom's bed:

Claire: How are you today, Tom?

Tom: Very low... (*short pause*)... Can't keep this drip in. I'm so thin, and the veins are gone.This keeps falling out, and you nurses have to keep putting it back – really gets me down. I'm glad you came. There is some bowel problem. I'm so thin – can't keep food in me.

Claire: You are very down today, Tom (*places a comforting hand on Tom's shoulder*) and the bowel is still a problem.

Tom: Yes, the dietician comes – she helped me pick the right food but I only pick at it. (*Pause*) I'm fed up of this colostomy. My father died last year ....

Tom grieved his losses, past and present.

As the days passed, Tom weakened. He felt very sad now as he contemplated his impending losses – his loss of life, of family, of role and function as husband and father. He was silent much of the time now. He prayed a lot. He appreciated those whose visits were brief and quiet, those who held his hand,listened to his sadness or just remainded silent.

Tom and Helen had struggled much. During these last days they accepted that Tom's life on earth would soon end. Tom was more peaceful in the expectation of it now. He was tired and weak. He dosed off to sleep often ... more often and for longer periods as time went on. Only his family was with him now. They were distraught. They held hands with him, prayed with him and spoke gently, reassuring him that he would not be alone. By taking turns they ensured that someone was with him all the time. Every time she left the room, Helen traced the Sign of the Cross on his forehead. All were careful about what they said even when he seemed to be asleep or unconscious.

When Tom died, Helen, Tomás, Sheila and Seán were at his bedside. Mary, unfortunately, was out at the time. Father Pat was there and prayed with them. One of the staff nurses was there. As Tom died peacefully Helen and the others said good-bye. They were heartbroken. Their being able to say good-bye, allowing him to go, and their acceptance will make their grief more bearable.

CHAPTER TWO

Reflecting on the Journey

How did they help?

Having travelled with Tom on his last journey, let us take a closer look at the whole experience. Initially both Tom and Helen denied the seriousness of the illness. Their close relatives shared this denial. Early on Helen insisted that Tom see another doctor also. She was hoping for a different diagnosis, hoping that there was a mistake of some kind. Not wanting or not able to believe the bad news, she told people that Tom was 'much better, thank you'. Or, in hope, she sometimes said such things as, 'doesn't he look better today, nurse?' They denied the truth, or put it temporarily out of their minds, until they could cope with it. When someone brings bad news isn't our first reaction to exclaim 'Oh, no!'? The diagnosis of a serious illness and/or the possibility of death so frightens and overwhelms us that at first we deny its reality or possibility. This is our way of coping at the time. It is a necessary and a healthy way of dealing with painful news. However, it is usually only a temporary defence.

The denial soon gave way to a new reaction – anger. Tom was lucky enough to be helped by understanding people, his friend Joe, and Father Pat, the hospital chaplain. It is worth noting the responses of these two people in the conversations quoted. They convey an understanding of what it must be like for Tom. The responses reflect the feeling and content of what Tom said:

I feel terrible. The nurses hurt me. I wouldn't treat anyone like this, not even a dog. They don't seem to realise that I had a big operation a few days ago.

And Joe responded:

Gosh, you are very cross with some of the nurses, Tom. You say they hurt you.

This allowed Tom the freedom to express his anger further and he went on:

They don't understand. I think I'll ring Helen to come and take me out of here. (*short pause*) The bloody doctor hardly ever shows up. See this thing, (*pointing to the drip*) it's bleeding now, but they won't fix it – they'll fool around until it's time to go and leave it to the next shift. The morning shift is very bad. They put this tube in me. I don't need any tube – never had one in my life. They are just too lazy to take me to the toilet.

During Father Pat's visit, Tom said:

Why did this god-damn thing have to happen to me anyway? Why? Why? On top of everything else at that? They just keep saying the same thing - wait, wait, wait. Just two weeks now, just two weeks now. What am I supposed to do? – look up at the ceiling for two weeks? They tell me that when I urinate, then I'll know I'm O.K., but when, when, when?

And Father Pat responded:

I know you must feel very angry Tom. This kidney thing is an added burden and two weeks sounds like an eternity.

Again, Tom was allowed the freedom to be angry and he went on:

> Yeh, and they treat me like a child - do this, do that, wait. What am I going to do? I have to do something about this.

As the conversation unfolded, Tom felt free to express what he needed to say.

Joe's and Father Pat's responses were helpful. They indicated an understanding and acceptance of Tom as he was at the time. They were non-judgemental and non-argumentative.

Relatives may also be angry. Again it may be directed at the doctor who made the diagnosis, who told the news, at any staff member, at the general practitioner, at the priest, at God or even at one another. At one time, Helen lashed out at Mr Curtin who made the diagnosis and told her the bad news.

Tom hoped to postpone the inevitable. He asked to live until Tomás could take over his drapery shop and until Seán made his Confirmation. Tom wanted to live. The family also made bargains but secretly.

But Tom's bargaining was short-lived and soon gave way to feelings of sadness over his losses. At first this was sadness over past and present losses like the loss of ability to do the things he always did. Dr Elizabeth Kübler-Ross calls this 'reactive depression'. Claire, the nurse who sat by his bed, understood. Tom expressed his sadness and grief:

> (I am) very low. (*pause*) Can't keep this drip in. I'm so thin, and the veins are gone. This keeps falling out, and you nurses have to keep putting it back – really gets me down. I'm glad you came. There is some bowel problem. I'm so thin – can't keep the food in me'.

Claire knew exactly how he felt:

> You are very down today, Tom, (*places a comforting hand on Tom's shoulder*) and the bowel is still a problem.

This allowed Tom the freedom to stay with the sadness he felt. It helped him grieve the losses he needed to grieve (his present loss of health, his Dad's death of a year ago) and then move on to prepare further for his leaving of this world.

As time passed Tom became more preoccupied with the losses ahead of him – the loss of life, of relatives, of function as husband, parent and brother. This was a lonely and silent time. Dr Kübler-Ross refers to it as 'preparatory depression' and feels that it is a necessary preparation for leaving this world in a state of acceptance and peace. The family quite wisely, and in their turns, stayed with him during this time.

Helen and the children, as well as Tom's brothers and sisters, felt a keen sense of loss and sadness also. Those who, at this time, were able to express their sadness and grief regarding their forthcoming loss, were better able to bear their loss later.

A conflict sometimes arises when the patient says, 'I know I have only a short time to live, but don't tell my husband/wife – he/she couldn't take it'. And the spouse speaks in similar words. Some help may be needed to break down the barrier. Both are relieved if and when this is done and they can talk freely.

We saw that Tom and Helen experienced various and different fears. This is very normal. It is helpful if those in the caring professions, and those who visit the sick and dying, understand these fears, accept them and help people cope with them. This means being able to sit and listen to them and being comfortable and relaxed doing so. So often a gentle touch or the sincere stroke of a hand, conveys support and acceptance.

When Tom was close to death, he had found peace and acceptance and was ready to die. It was most important that Helen and the other family members understood this acceptance. They understood that Tom had found peace and was ready to die. In his last days Tom asked to be visited by only a few and finally only by Helen and/or his children or by Helen alone. This was normal and healthy detachment. We are pleased when someone reaches this state of peace. And particularly so when the family members understand it. Otherwise there may be a painful conflict when the patient is ready to die and family members are unable to accept, say good-bye and allow their loved one to go. Needless to say, this is an extremely difficult and painful thing to do. At this time the family needs the most support. It is often helpful to explain what is happening and the possible conflict to the family members, at the right-time.

We cherish our customs of placing a crucifix in the hand and making the Sign of the Cross on the forehead of a dying person. They indicate our belief that Christ, by his Cross, triumphed over death. We believe that, like Christ, this person will pass through death to a life where death does not exist – the life of the Resurrection.

When someone dies, he or she is at peace, but for the family the struggle goes on. They continue, or begin, their journey through bereavement.

Hope throughout the journey

Studies indicate that hope persists right through serious illness. Even the most accepting patients hope for a remission, a cure, the discovery of a new drug, or a miracle. Dr Elizabeth Kübler-Ross, in *On Death and Dying*, quotes a fifty-three year old man suffering from a cancerous skin disorder:

'Somewhere someone is going to do research. There are a lot of good brains working on this condition. They might even discover a cure while in the process of working on something else. I hope that some morning I will sit up on the other side of the bed, and the doctor will be there, and he will say, 'I want to give you this injection'. And in a few days my skin will clear up and I will go back to work.'

Dr Kübler-Ross found that when hope was dropped in a state of final acceptance, death was close. People may say such things as, 'I won't be around much longer.' One patient who always believed in a miracle eventually said, 'I think this is the miracle – I am ready now and not afraid any more.'

When a patient expresses hope of a remission, cure or whatever, we should share this hope with them. There is a painful conflict when the staff or family communicate a sense of hopelessness to a patient who desperately needs hope.

For a christian, surely all the 'little hopes' of the dying person are pointers to the great hope of eternal life in heaven.

Who can help a sick or dying person?

The patient must be allowed to make his/her own choice of who can best help at a particular time. He/she chooses to whom he/she talks, in whom he/she confides. A certain patient had inoperable metastatic cancer, had several hospital stays, innumerable unpleasant tests, useless noxious medication, was cut open and cut open again, relieved of her uterus, her ovaries, lower body circulation and some lung tissues. At one time she indicated that a particular staff nurse was the best relief in her agony because she was a person to whom she was 'able to talk about death without burdening someone who really cared for me'. 'I could talk to her about death', she said, 'something the others refused to do. Having spoken, I was better able to think, the brain was less cluttered.'

Anyone can help a sick or dying person. The basic need of a dying person until the last moment is for a human being who can be sensitive to his/her needs, who can listen, is compassionate, and is relaxed in his/her presence. The most one can give is oneself.

The best help is given by those who have understood and worked through the feelings and emotions associated with dying and who have come to understand and accept the future fact of their own death.

Death
It is very difficult, many would say impossible, for us to imagine our own death. The statement, 'I shall one day die' is a bit too specific for comfort. There is the story of a married couple who agreed that when one of them died, the other would mourn for only so long, and then use the insurance money to travel. Sometime later the husband was heard to remark: 'Do you know what I was thinking just now? When one of us dies, I think I'll go to Paris'.

In our unconscious mind we are immortal.

25

Death is something that only happens to others. Nevertheless it 'is always looming somewhere in the background and we're not sure what to do about it. Should we approach it as part of life or put it away until it approaches us? One thing is certain – we cannot avoid it.' For the atheist, it is the end. For the agnostic, it is confusing. For the christian, it is the gateway to eternal life, the life of the Resurrection. Its meaning is based on the death of Jesus. On Good Friday Jesus gave himself completely to the Father in death. The Father then raised him to the new life of the Resurrection. From the moment of death we can share in the life of the Resurrection. Christ said: 'I am the Resurrection'[1] and he promised, 'because you believe in me you will live forever in heaven, where no eye has seen nor ear heard, nor has it entered into the heart of man what things God has prepared for those that love him.'[2]

Our unconscious mind is correct. We are immortal. The Preface of the Requiem Mass states: 'Lord, for your faithful people, life is changed not ended.' The God who gives life does not suddenly cut it off. Death is a step towards a fuller life with him. We cannot deny the fact that there is a radical break between this life and the next. But we believe that it is a continuation of our journey towards God. On earth we believe in God through faith. In heaven we will be with him.

Dr Elizabeth Kübler-Ross came to the same conclusion. In the Foreword to *FreeFall*[3] by JoAnn Kelley Smith, a dying person, she wrote, 'Those of us who have studied what happens to people at the moment they die know that death does not really exist. Only the physical body dies. If you could have listened to those who have died – medically speaking – but made a comeback, you would know that there is no need to fear.'

There is the story told about an elderly man in the west of Ireland. After he had learned that he was dying of an incurable cancer, a friend rang him to say how sorry he was to hear the bad news. 'What bad news?' he asked, 'This is what I have been preparing for all my life.'

1. Jn 11:25
2. 1 Cor 2: 9
3. Kelley Smith, JoAnn, *Free Fall*, Judson Press (1975) & SPCK, London(1977).

CHAPTER THREE

How to help

We journeyed with Tom and his family through the illness that eventually led to his death. We noted the different feelings, emotions and struggles they experienced. An understanding of the struggles which people experience, and coping mechanisms which we use with serious illness and/or impending death, may help us to be sensitive to and understanding of the needs of someone who is sick or dying. It is vital also that we be aware of the affect on ourselves.

The following summary and guidelines may be helpful:

Disclosure:
The patient is told or knows somehow.
In the beginning, hope,
which is always present, is for cure.

1. State of Denial:
The refusal to believe that one has a terminal illness.
'Not me, the diagnosis must be wrong.'
It is a healthy shock-absorber.

Do:
Remember that the need for denial exists in every patient at times but more so at the beginning of a serious illness.

Don't:
Don't encourage denial.

Listen patiently, not confirming or denying statements – the patient may need this time to adjust mentally – let the facts speak for themselves.

Allow defences – don't point out contradictions.

Sustain realistic hope in order to prevent a sense of abandonment.

Be alert for prolonged denial.

2. Anger

Starting to accept the inevitable but feeling angry at self, relatives, medical and hospital personnel who are healthy and at God who allows him/her to die. ('Why me?')

Do:

Try to understand by imagining self in the same position.

Allow and help patient to express anger – then he/she will realise that he/she is cared for.

Visit regularly.

Don't:

Don't argue.
Don't judge.
Don't take personally.

Don't abandon patient.

3. Bargaining
An attempt to postpone.

Do:
Join in the bargaining
— help to be realistic in
the bargaining.

In the further stages, hope is not so much a seeking for a cure but a search for meaning in what is happening.

4. Depression
Sadness and a sense of great loss.

(a) Reactive depression:
*Sadness over past and present losses,
e.g. job, bodily organs.*

Do:

Listen patiently.

Help in meeting unmet
responsibilities.

Boost self-esteem by
praise.

Don't:

Don't abandon.

(b) Preparatory Depression:
*Sense of sadness over impending loss of life,
of significant relationships and significant roles.
Necessary to prepare for final state of
Acceptance and Peace.*

Do:	Don't:
Be there - then he/she knows he/she is not forgotten.	
Allow expression of sorrow.	Don't encourage him/her to look on the bright side – this would hinder contemplation of impending death.
Support search for meaning - make sense out of it all.	

5. Acceptance
A time of peace – 'void of feelings'.

Do:
Explain this stage to family – help them to 'let go'.
Touch.
Prayer.

6. Fulfillment
'I'm ready to go now'.

Fears

A seriously sick and/or dying person
may experience various fears and anxieties such as:

Do:

Fear of the unknown:
What lies ahead?
'I have never died before.'
The dying process.
Afterlife.

Be present.
Listen.
Understand.
Touch.
Care.

Fear of loneliness/
alienation.

Visit/listen.

Fear of lack of
acceptance: Somehow
feeling less a person or
unequal or different
because of the malady
or disease.

Accept:
Sit and listen and be
relaxed and comfortable
doing so.
-Understand.
Touch conveys equality
Empathy (understand-
ing, in so far as it is possible, what it is like for
the patient and letting
him/her feel free to feel
what he/she feels and
express it as he/she
wishes, e.g. in anger; in
tears.

Fear of loss of dignity:
Bed skipped on medical
round.
Subject avoided.

Treat as normal, doing
all usual things, bring-
ing the normal news –
this prevents loss of
individuality and gives a
sense of normality.

Fear of loss of independence:	Accept Understand
Fear of unkown about medical condition:	Truth (information relieves anxiety).
Fear of pain:	Reassurance

Our task is to stay with people in their fear and free them. They are living persons – living towards death as you and I are, even if we are at a different stage of the journey. Always treat them as the living persons they are.

The Dying Person's Bill of Rights

1.
I have the right to be treated as a living human being
until I die.

2.
I have the right to maintain
a sense of hopefulness,
however changing its focus may be.

3.
I have the right to be cared for
by those who can maintain a sense of hopefulness,
however changing this might be.

4.
I have the right to express my feelings and emotions
about my approaching death in my own way.

5.
I have the right to participate in decisions
concerning my care.

6.
I have the right to expect
continuing medical and nursing attention
even though 'cure' goals
must be changed to 'comfort' goals.
I have a right to be free from pain.

7.
I have the right to have my questions
answered honestly.

8.
I have the right to be cared for
by caring, sensitive, knowledgeable people
who will attempt to understand my needs
and will be able to gain some satisfaction
in helping me face my death.

9.
I have the right not to be deceived.

10.
I have the right to have help
from and for my family
in accepting my death.

11.
I have the right to discuss and enlarge
my religious and/or spiritual experiences,
whatever these may mean to others.

12.
I have the right to retain my individuality
and not to be judged for my decisions
which may be contrary to the beliefs of others.

13.
I have the right to die in peace and dignity.

14.
I have the right not to die alone.

15.
I have the right to expect
that the sanctity of my human body
will be respected after death.

Adapted from Donovan, M.I., and Pierce, S.G.,
Cancer Care Nursing,
New York, Appleton-Century-Crofts,
1976

CHAPTER FOUR

The Passion, Death and Resurrection of Jesus

Tom suffered a serious illness which eventually led to his death. While each person will cope in his/her own unique way, many experience similar feelings and emotions. It is interesting to look at the Gospel accounts of Jesus' Passion and Death and see how Jesus coped with his impending death.

Let us begin by assuming that Jesus knew that his journey to Jerusalem for the celebration of the Passover was his last journey. On Palm Sunday Jesus rode triumphantly into Jerusalem. It must have been difficult for him to believe that his death was close as he was praised and affirmed by so many. He must have felt, 'No, not me.' We can almost hear him say, 'It can't be.'

A few days later, on Holy Thursday, in the Garden of Gethsemane, Jesus asked Peter, James and John to stay near him. He said: 'My soul is sorrowful to the point of death. Wait here and stay awake with me.'(*Mt 26:38*) Feeling alone and isolated he needed the presence of another human being as he faced death. He checked three times to be reassured by their presence and support. But they slept.

Also in the Garden Jesus said, 'Father, if it be possible, take this cup from me.'(*Mt 26:39*) However, this request passes quickly. The bargaining isn't accepted and Jesus moves towards accepting his death, 'Let your will be done, not mine.'(*Lk*

22:42) (We remember that people move in and out of different feelings and emotions again and again).

And there was the time in the Garden when, away from his apostles and in silence, he knelt and prayed as he prepared for his impending death. (*Preparatory depression*).

As Jesus made his way to Calvary, he met the women of Jerusalem 'who mourned and lamented for him.'(*Lk 23:47*) There was anger in his words as he spoke, "Daughters of Jerusalem, do not weep for me: weep rather for yourselves and for your children. For the days will surely come when people will say,'Happy are those who are barren, the wombs that never bore, the breasts that have never suckled.' Then they will begin to say to the mountains, 'Fall on us,' to the hills, 'Cover us.' For if men use the green wood like this, what will happen when it is dry."(*Lk 23: 28-31*)

This kind of anger is not unlike that expressed to doctors, nurses, clergy, other hospital personnel, family members or at God. It is not because of who they are but because I am dying and I am envious of those who are escaping it, at least for now.

How angry and depressed Jesus must have been when, on the Cross, he felt abandoned even by God. He cried out, 'My God, my God, why have you forsaken me?'(*Mk 15:34*) (Many people facing death feel at some stage that everyone has abandoned them, even God).

But Jesus' final acceptance was also expressed on the Cross as he was about to die and he was able to say: 'Father, into your hands, I commit my spirit.' (*Lk 23:46*)

On that first Good Friday, Jesus gave himself to the Father in death. Three days later, the Father raised him to the glory of the Resurrection.

To those who believe in him, particularly those who share his Passion, the promise of Christ will be fulfilled – 'I am the Resurrection.'(*Jn 11:25*) 'Because you believed in me you will never die, but will live forever in heaven,"where no eye has seen, nor ear heard, nor has it entered into the heart of man what things God has prepared for those who love him."' (*1 Cor 2:9*)

PART II

Bereavement

CHAPTER FIVE

Bereavement: The Journey

The Background

'The statistics about death are quite impressive: one out of one people dies.' (*G.B. Shaw*) Since death follows life and grief follows death, grief is experienced by everyone. The only way one could escape is never to love, because 'the pain of grief is the price of love'.

Grief is the emotional reaction to loss – the complex of emotions we feel when we lose someone or something about whom or about which we care deeply. It is not limited to death. Loss of a limb, loss of job, a broken marriage, loss of a friend and all personal losses result in grief.

Bereavement is the sense of loss and grief we feel after the death of a loved person. It is one of the most intense emotional experiences in life. It is the greatest source of sadness. When we lose someone we love, we lose part of ourselves.

> *A gentle Father*
> *and the God of all consolation*
> *who comforts us*
> *in all our sorrows.*
>
> *2 Cor 1: 3-4*

The grief experience is as old as mankind, and in recent years it has been studied closely. It is now believed that there is a 'grief cycle', that is, various identifiable feelings and emotions consistent with the grief process. These are particular emotional responses which, if coped with, help the person eventually to accept the death and adjust to new life. They may include:

1. Numbness/Shock and/or Denial
2. Emotional Release
3. Pining - Searching
4. Loneliness - Depression - Sadness
5. Sense of Guilt
6. Anger
7. Resistance
8. Hope
9. Recovery

Again note the following two points:

(i) Everyone does not necessarily move through these emotions one after the other. They move to and fro; some may be present together; others may never be present.

(ii) Certain factors make a difference to the intensity and duration of the grief experience, factors such as:
   - the strength of the attachment,
   - the timeliness or the untimeliness of the loss,
   - the available support,
   - personal factors, *eg* previous psychological illness,
   - with regard to the death of a child, the depth of the loss experienced will relate in some degree to the age of the child.

Here, we follow the experience of one family but the feelings and emotions described are universal.

The Journey

When Tom died, Helen, Tomás, Mary, Sheila and Seán, as well as Tom's brothers and sisters, were left to mourn their loss. In a sense they had already begun their grief journey as they anticipated Tom's death. Still, they experienced a deep sense of finality when Tom died. Now they have to adjust to the new situation. We will follow their journey through a series of selected letters. These are some of Helen's letters, at different times, as the family journeyed through their grief. They indicate some of the different feelings and emotions which are part of grief. Some are written to Father Pat, the hospital chaplain, whom they got to know during Tom's visits to the hospital and whose support they accepted and appreciated. Others are to Catherine, a close personal friend. Helen and Catherine had kept contact over the years despite their being living in different counties now.

Numbness–Denial–Loneliness

12th March

Dear Father Pat,

I am writing on behalf of all our family to thank you for your help and support during Tom's last illness. I am so glad that you were with us when he died. Your presence, our prayers together, and your helping us to allow him go at the end made it easier for us. I miss Tom very much. The pain of being without him is terrible. I was hopeful until very near the end. I think now that if I had realised at the time of his death and funeral (three weeks ago today) how much I would miss him, I would not have been able to cope. Mary is very upset as she was very close to her father. I felt so sorry for her when she arrived late and couldn't realise that her Daddy had just died. I can still see her there holding him and shouting 'Wake up, Daddy, wake up, talk to me'.

I'm glad that you were able to say the funeral Mass. He would have wanted you.

It is hard to face ordering the mortuary cards. I couldn't believe it when I saw the samples in the post on the day of the burial. No one had even thought of them, let alone order them. It really brought home the facts to me. Why do they do that? It seems so cruel?

When I was in town yesterday, I met the nurse who was with us when Tom died. She was great. I felt her support as she joined in the prayer with us and made every effort to see that Tom was comfortable. She was very helpful with the phone calls afterwards.

I will finish for now, Father Pat. It helps when I share my thoughts and feelings.My friend and neighbour, Irene, is very good and calls regularly. I am very lonely, Father. Please call when you get a chance.

Regards,

Helen

19th April

Dear Father Pat,

I was so glad to see you the other day. I'm sorry for crying so much but I needed to. Thank you for being there. I went to Mass in St John's on Sunday and the priest spoke of Jesus weeping at the grave of Lazarus, his friend. I was consoled by the words, which I think I will always remember: 'History's most perfect man stood by the graveside and wept. Tears are neither masculine or feminine. They are human.' Tomás was with me. He didn't say anything, but I know it helped him. It reminded me again of the nurse who allowed me to cry at Tom's bedside. Too many people have advised me to stop crying and upsetting myself. They don't understand how much I need to cry at times. They just don't seem to be comfortable if I cry.

Again thanks for being there when I needed you. You have been a great help. Please call again sometime.

Regards,

Helen.

10th May,

Dear Catherine,
The days are getting longer, and I'm getting sadder.
I think of Tom all the time. I remember our walks together in the summer evenings, the evenings we
spent watching T.V., going for a drink at week-ends.
We talked about everything, and shared our worries
about our children. Everywhere I go, every song I
hear, everywhere I look, reminds me of him. I
treasure the watch he gave me for my birthday, also
his rosary beads and so many other little things. I
have photographs put away safely. It is too painful
for me to look at them yet.I go to his grave almost
every day. How I wish everything to be as it was.

There are so many new things I have to do that I
never did before – paying the bills, locking the
doors at night. I find it so hard. I hurt so much inside
right now, I wonder how long I can carry on. I don't
know if I will ever adjust to being a widow. Tom was
such a loving and kind person. People tell me that
time heals. I hope and pray that it does. So often I
feel that God has deserted me. Even though I feel
very close to Tom, I realise now that we will never
meet on this earth again.

It all seems so final but it helps to write and tell
someone who understands. I hope to see you
soon, Catherine.

God Bless for now.

Helen.

22nd July

Dear Father Pat,

Thank you for taking the time to visit me again last week. The reassurance that my reactions and feelings are normal has lifted a weight from me. The reflection 'Footprints' that you gave me is beautiful. When I read it, it reassures me that God is still with me. Were it not for prayer, I think I would not be able to cope.

I was very upset the other evening. Tomás got so cross that it frightened me. I don't know what came over him. He cursed the doctor who treated his father. He said he wouldn't go to Mass or pray anymore. He said it hadn't been much use to his father or to me. I tried to tell him how much it helps me to know that God is with me and helping me. That only made things worse. He said he could not and did not want to speak to God. His father had been the kind of person God wants us to be – kind and loving. So why did he suffer so much? Why is death so final, so cruel and unkind? I told you how cross I was myself in the early weeks after Tom's death. At times I still get bitter and ask if God can be so cruel. But it's not as bad now. I know Tomás feels very bitter right now, but I try to help him and let him talk.

Thank you for explaining and reassuring me that we are not all going mad.

Best wishes,

Helen.

Footprints

One night a man had a dream. He dreamed he was walking along the beach with the Lord. Across the sky flashed scenes from his life.

For each scene, he noticed two sets of footprints in the sand ... one belonging to him and the other to the Lord.

When the last scene of his life flashed before him, he looked back at the footprints in the sand. He noticed that many times along the path of his life there was only one set of footprints. He also noticed that it happened at the very lowest and saddest times of his life.

This really bothered him and he questioned the Lord about it: 'Lord, you said that once I decided to follow you, you'd walk with me all the way. But I have noticed that during the most troublesome times in my life, there is only one set of footprints. I don't understand why, when I needed you most, you would leave me.'

The Lord replied, 'My precious, precious child, I love you and I would never leave you during your times of trial and suffering. When you see only one set of footprints, it was then that I carried you.'

Guilt

31st August

Dear Father Pat,

I would like to come and see you soon. Right now I feel so guilty about some things that I want to talk to you. I am sorry for being cranky at times. I am sorry I didn't tell Tom more often how much I loved him and appreciated him. I hope he knew. I worry now about some things done and other things not done, about words said or left unsaid. There are a few things especially about which I want to talk to you. I'll ring you before the next day I go to town.

The children are going back to school tomorrow. It is hard for them to be without their Daddy but they seem to be as well as could be expected. Tomás did very well in his Leaving, despite the hard year he had. He got three honours. He is in the shop full-time now and seems to be doing well. Mike, his uncle is a good teacher of business.

God bless. I hope to see you soon.

Helen.

Anniversary

6th February

Dear Father Pat,
Tom's anniversary is in two weeks time. I would like
you to say the anniversary Mass. This is a difficult
time for me. I feel I am living through those last
weeks of his life again. It's the loneliness that is the
worst, Father. Christmas was very lonely. Please let
me know the time of the Mass. We will all be there.
I look forward to hearing from you.

All the best,

Helen.

> *We want you to be quite certain*
> *about those who have died*
> *to make sure you do not grieve about them,*
> *like the other people who have no hope.*
> *We believe that Jesus died and rose again, and*
> *that it will be the same*
> *for those who have died in Jesus:*
> *God will bring them with him.*
> *With such thoughts as these*
> *you should comfort one another.*
>
> *(1 Thess 4:13-14,18)*

14th October

Dear Catherine,
I seem to be coping a bit better now, thank God. I enjoy going out with my friends. Christmas will be lonely again, but I will get strength from knowing that the Son of God is with me.

I am grateful to those who invited me out and encouraged me to do things again. At first I found it strange being out without Tom. I didn't want to go. I was afraid of being disloyal to him or allowing his memory to fade. I know for certain now that that can never happen. Life will never be the same but it goes on and I can live again. I look forward to going to you for a few days after Christmas but we'll be in touch before that.

Bye for now,

Helen.

Conclusion
St Paul advised us to allow ourselves and others to grieve, but in a healthy way and with hope – a hope and faith that 'life is changed, not ended'; and in the knowledge:
   that love given cannot be taken back;
   that love is stronger than death;
   that we can help our loved ones and they can help us, because we are all one in Christ,
   and they share the glory to which we look forward, the glory of the Resurrection.

CHAPTER SIX

How to help the Grieving

The feelings, emotions and reactions which Helen and her children experienced in the months after Tom's death were not untypical. An understanding of this aspect of grief may help us to be sensitive to the needs of someone who is grieving. It should also help us in our own grief.

The following summary and guidelines may be helpful:

1. State of Shock/Numbness and/or Denial
A temporary anaesthesia or escape from reality.
Lasts from a few minutes to a few days.

Do:
Say you are sorry about what happened and about their pain.

Don't:
Don't say you know how they feel (unless you have had similar experience, you probably don't know how they feel. Everyone's grief is unique).

Be available to help: listen, do messages, make calls; give information about what to do, who to contact re: funeral arrangements;

Don't take away what the person is able to do.

Attend to material things *e.g.* food; in a quiet way do what you see to be the need.

Help them adjust to the reality of death by using the language of death. Encourage them to view the body if they haven't already done so.

Don't support denial.

Allow them to express the grief they are feeling and are willing to share.

Let your genuine concern and caring show.

Don't let your own sense of inadequacy, helplessness, and discomfort keep you from them.

Reassure them that they did everything that they could, that the medical care their relative received was the best and whatever else you know to be true and positive about the care given.

Don't make any comments which suggest that the care given at home, in the Accident/ Emergency Room, hospital or wherever was inadequate.(They may feel enough doubt and guilt without it being added to).

2. Emotional Release

Do:
Allow tears and expression of emotions – we have tear glands to use when we have good reason to use them.

Don't:
Don't tell them to stop upsetting themselves or to stop crying.

3. Searching/Pining

Thoughts about the deceased preoccupy the mind 'Her absence is like the sky, spread over everything.'[1]

4. Depression–Loneliness–Sadness

It is a universal experience.
The feeling that God does not care.

Don't:
Don't say 'you ought to be feeling better by now', or anything else which implies a judgement about their feelings.

Don't tell them what they should feel or do.

5. Sense of Guilt

(a) Normal Guilt: We have done something, or neglected to do something, for which we ought to feel guilty? Need for forgiveness. Forgive yourself.
(b) Neurotic Guilt:
Feeling guilty
out of proportion to the real situation.

Do: Allow expression.

6. Anger
A normal part of the grief process.

Do:	*Don't:*
Allow expression.	Don't take personally.
Assure that this is normal.	
Affirm that God will continue to help them. Allow God to be part of the solution, not part of the problem.	Don't give pat answers – religious or otherwise. (*e.g.* 'will of God' or 'angel in heaven'.)

7. Resistance
Feeling a resistance to return
to the normal routine of life.
Feeling that one's task is to keep the memory
of the loved one alive.

Do: Allow people to talk about the loved one.

8. Hope
Grief may last from a few weeks to many months.
Now and then we get a glimpse of hope
in something or other.

9. Recovery
Acceptance of the reality of changed circumstances.
Affirmation that life can still be worth living.
Life goes on, not as before, but differently.

Do: Encourage people
to take up activities and relationships
while not forcing them to do so.

At all times:

Do:
Be there/available.

Allow people to talk about the deceased as much and as often as they want to.

Don't:

Don't change the subject when they mention the deceased.

Children:

Do:
Bring them to the funeral.

Reassure them that the family will stay together and affirm that they will continue to be cared for.

Don't:

Don't avoid mentioning the deceased person's name out of fear of reminding them of their pain. (They haven't forgotten it.)

Don't lie to them. Don't say things like 'he is gone to sleep.' (May create fear of going to sleep) or 'God took him.' (Creates a wrong image of God).

Don't put too much responsibility on them (expecting them to take over role of deceased) – creates fear.

Confidentiality

Defences may be low at the time of death, during bereavement or during hospitalisation. People may disclose more than usual, *e.g.* family rows, relationships etc. Be careful to respect and preserve confidentiality.

To help others

Many people find it difficult to support those who are grieving: they find it painful to listen to another's grief – especially if they have unresolved sorrows of their own. But it should help to:

(i)   have a general knowledge of the feelings and emotions consistent with grief.

(ii) realise that it is natural and must run its course.

(iii) remember that 'grief cannot be cured, but can be shared', so listen and allow expression of feeling and emotion.

To prepare oneself for grief

(i)   Be aware of the process and have a general knowledge of it. The hurt is lessened if you understand what is happening.

(ii) Love now – be kind now – say what you want to say now – then you will have no regrets. We shouldn't wait until they can't hear us to express our love; we shouldn't wait until they can't smell them to bring our flowers.

(iii) Have the God revealed in Jesus Christ as the centre of your life.

1. C.S. Lewis, *A Grief Observed*, Faber Paperback, (1961), P.13.

PART III

Stillbirth and Neo-Natal Death

CHAPTER SEVEN

Stillbirth

Carol and Jack O'Connor were happy and content in expectation of their second baby. Their son, Paul, was four years old and they were delighted in anticipation of a little brother or sister for him. They were quite excited as Carol entered the last month of her pregnancy.

Then one day she thought she didn't feel any life. She went to see Dr O'Shea. Carol saw the worry in the doctor's face and pleaded with her to find the heartbeat. Dr O'Shea referred Carol to the hospital. As Jack drove they sat in silence most of the way, fearing the worst. At the hospital their worst fears were confirmed. Their baby was dead and would be stillborn. Carol went to pieces. Jack did his best to support her but he was shocked and in bits also. The staff in the maternity ward were very supportive and helpful to both of them and this support and assistance was to last right through Carol's stay in the hospital. The day after baby Niamh died, Kay McCarthy, the ward sister, advised that Paul might visit Carol. Mr O'Donnell, the obstetrician, was very kind also and answered all their questions. Father Pat, the hospital chaplain, was a good support. They sensed that he understood and appreciated the pain they felt.

Carol and Jack's baby was stillborn at nine o'clock the following evening. Next day her friend, Anne, visited her. Carol was sitting on a chair at the bedside. Her expression was sad:

Anne: Carol, I'm so sorry. (*Anne places her hand on Carol's shoulder*)

Carol: I know, Anne. My baby was born this morning. Mam told you about me?

Anne: Yes.

Carol: (*Crying*) I'm sorry, Anne.

Anne: It's alright Carol. You can cry. (*Places a comforting hand on Carol's shoulder*) (*Pause*)

Carol: (*crying*) Oh, Anne, I don't know why this happened to me. The doctors should have been able to do more. God is so cruel. I'm so angry, Anne.

Anne: Oh I know, Carol – angry with God and with the doctors?

Carol: I am. Haven't I every right to be. I was looking forward so much to my baby. I don't know if I'll ever pray again... (*crying*)

Anne: You can be angry, Carol. You are hurting a lot. And it's hard to pray when God seems so far away. (*Anne embraces Carol*)

Carol: Oh, I ache. (*Crying*) (*Pause*) I didn't do anything bad enough to deserve this. And what's worse, I feel I have failed Jack. He was looking forward so much to this baby too.

Anne: Oh Carol. (*Anne puts her arms around Carol*) I know it's painful to feel that. And to be blaming yourself.

Carol: (*Crying*) Thank you for understanding, Anne. You are a real friend.

Later:

Carol: There is something else I'm wondering about, Anne. I don't know if I want to see our baby or not. I didn't look after it was born, though the nurse asked me. Jack says he doesn't want to see it. Mr O'Donnell was in this morning. He encouraged me to see it.

Anne: You are wondering what's the right thing to do?

Carol: When Dad died, I came just after and didn't realise he was dead... (*Pause*)... I don't know what to do.

Anne: Is it that you want to see your baby, but are half afraid?

Carol: I suppose that's it.

Anne: What's your baby's name, Carol?

Carol: Niamh. (*tears*) Nurse Daly baptised her as she was born.

After a while Carol realised that she would probably regret not availing of the opportunity to see and hold Niamh. Referring to her as Niamh was helpful. She felt that she would like Jack to be with her when she went to see their baby.

Next day:
When Anne came Carol was lying in bed. Her expression was sad. When Anne entered the room, Carol cried immediately. Then she said:

> We went to see her, Jack and I. And we both held her. She was a perfect baby... (*tears*)... I'm so glad I saw her and held her. Now I can say 'her' and call her Niamh. We spent a long time with Niamh. And we went back again later. I think I will always cherish those times. Paul will see his little sister, too, if he wishes. One of the nurses gave me this booklet (*Carol shows the booklet to Anne*).

It is called *A Little Lifetime*.[1] It explains my feelings and what to expect. And about the post-mortem and funeral service. I'd like Father Pat, the chaplain here, to celebrate Mass. And I want to be there no matter what.

The funeral was arranged for the following day when Carol was discharged from hospital. After Mass in the hospital chapel, Jack and Carol brought the body of their little daughter to the cemetery and she was buried with her grandfather. Their families and friends were there to support them.

Some weeks later, Carol wrote to Anne:

17th September

Dear Anne,

I finally got round to writing. I am trying to pick up the pieces again, but still get very low at times. I still cry a lot for my baby girl. I was in bits the day she was due to be born. Jack is a great support. He feels very sad at times, too. I try to support him, as he does me. Thank God we understand one another and try to be sensitive to each other's feelings. I am so pleased that I went to Niamh's Mass and funeral. The Mass and prayers helped a lot. I treasure the keepsakes that I got at the hospital, especially the coloured photograph, the lock of hair, and Niamh's birth and baptismal certificate. Paul is back at school now, and excited about being in his new class. I'm glad he saw his baby sister, and said goodbye to her. He put one of his toys into Niamh's coffin and said goodbye in his own way. He is so lively: he keeps me busy.

It hurts me so much at times when people say

the wrong thing. I think I'll scream if someone talks to me again about an angel in heaven. I long to hold my own baby here on earth. When someone tells me I am young and can have other children, I feel like punching them. Others go to great lengths to talk about everything and anything except our loss of Niamh. They pretend that nothing ever happened. Some of them even crossed the street to avoid meeting me. One neighbour told her children not to call for a while, even though they always came to play with Paul. I feel so hurt and isolated when these things happen. In the supermarket I feel everyone is looking at me as if I were different. But, thankfully, most came and sympathised. That was helpful and it broke the ice for me. They acknowledged that I gave birth to a baby girl and sympathised with us because she died.

Thank God for a friend like you, Anne, who listens and allows me to talk about her or not, as I choose. Our curate called a few times. He is very helpful too.

I rang Mam last night. I know she grieves for me as well as for Niamh.

Again I want to thank you for your help, Anne.

Regards from Jack and Paul also.

Bye for now,

Carol.

1. *A Little Lifetime* is a booklet for parents whose babies have died around the time of birth, produced by the Irish Stillbirth and Neonatal Death Society.
The Irish Sudden Infant Death Association have also issued a booklet called *Cot Death,* dealing with questions like grief, guilt and the future after cot death.

CHAPTER EIGHT

Suggested Hospital Policy for Stillbirth and Neo-Natal Death

This policy emerged mainly from the advice of parents whose babies died around the time of birth.

Aims:
- (1) to make death real;
- (2) to recognise the family need;
- (3) to aid good grieving.

Pre-Delivery:
– inform parents together (if possible) of the facts of intra-uterine death or congenital abnormality not compatible with life;
– encourage them to be together for labour and delivery; -ask for a name for the baby;
– chaplain, doctor and nurses visit and give time to the parents together and/or individually;
– mother should not be left alone during labour.

When Intra-Uterine Death is confirmed during delivery:
(a)If the father is not already present, he should be contacted and encouraged to be present if at all possible;
(b)Parents to be informed of baby's death together if possible.

Post-Delivery:
- baptise and name baby;
- encourage the parents to see and hold baby;
- give the parents time alone with baby;
- take a photograph of baby;
- chaplain, doctor and nurses visit and give time to the parents together and/or individually;
- give the parents copy of *A Little Lifetime*;
- do the parents want a post-mortem? Will it help? Give them time to decide;
- ensure other children in the family get to see the mother as soon as possible;
- encourage them to allow time:
  for a change of mind;
  for the facts to sink in;
  for the mother to attend the funeral;
- arrange for the baby to be laid out according to the wishes of the parents;
- counsel the parents carefully on the question of a coffin for a physically deformed child, e.g. hydro-cephalus;
- encourage the parents to have a funeral service at the hospital and at the graveside. Include Mass, if they wish.(*The Roman Missal* contains the appropriate Mass and the *Lectionary* suggested readings.) Other family members, and members of the community, might be present. Bring other children.
- encourage the parents to bury the baby in an iden-tifiable family grave;
- give baptismal certificate to parents;
- inform G.P., Public Health Nurse and local clergy of the event.

When the Baby Dies in Neo-Natal Period:

- the parents should be encouraged to spend as much time as possible with the baby before death;
- handle sensitively the question of breast feeding if the death of baby is inevitable;
- a photograph should be taken;
- chaplain, doctor and nurses visit and give time to the parents together and/or individually;
- give the parents copy of *A Little Lifetime*.
- do the parents want a post-mortem? Will it help? Give them time to decide;
- ensure other children in the family get to see the mother as soon as possible;
- encourage them to allow time:
  for a change of mind;
  for the facts to sink in;
  for the mother to attend the funeral;
- arrange for the baby to be laid out according to the wishes of the parents;
- counsel the parents carefully on the question of a coffin for a physically deformed child, e.g. hydrocephalus;
- encourage the parents to have a funeral service at the hospital and at the graveside. Include Mass, if they wish.(*The Roman Missal* contains the appropriate Mass and the *Lectionary* suggested readings.) Other family members, and members of the community, might be present. Bring other children.
- encourage the parents to bury the baby in an identifiable family grave;
- give baptismal certificate to parents;
- inform G.P., Public Health Nurse and local clergy of the event.

At Post-Natal Check:
- parents should meet the consultant and anyone else they wish in order to assess and try to meet any needs. The meetings should be unhurried.
- make the post-mortem findings available, if any;
- make the photograph available, if not already obtained;
- encourage time for mourning before further pregnancy;
- if it is felt that parents are not progressing in their grief, perhaps further referral should be made.

CHAPTER NINE

Baptism and Stillbirth, Miscarriage and Neo-Natal Death

The Sacrament of Baptism formally attaches us to Christ and to his Church. As members of the Church we are entitled to receive the other sacraments and share fully in the life of the Church. At baptism, parents publicly undertake their responsibility to bring up their new son or daughter as a Catholic and prepare him/her for the other sacraments, especially Reconciliation, Eucharist and Confirmation. They also undertake to teach him/her the essential Christian virtues of truth, honesty, respect etc.

There are some who, unfortunately, through no fault of their own or of anyone else, are unable to formally receive baptism with water – miscarried or stillborn infants, or babies who die suddenly and unexpectedly.

Holy Scripture and the official law of the Church teach that these children are with God. The faith and desire of their parents, of the Church, and the mercy of God ensure this. The Scripture advocates faith and trust in the mercy of God. The official law of the Church, the *Code of Canon Law*, in Canon 849, states:

> Baptism, the gateway to the sacraments, is necessary for salvation, either by actual reception, or at least by desire.

The grace of God (the pure gift of God) and the gift of faith come to us without merit on our part. They come merely because we do not reject them. From the moment of conception an infant is subject to the grace of God through the prayers of the Church. 'Today theologians still maintain the principle that we can only be saved by Christ through the Church, but they see the prayer of the Church as efficacious even when it cannot be ritually expressed in the sacrament. Thus it is very probable that the infant dying before baptism has already been justified through the prayer of the Church (especially of the child's family) and will enter into the intimate mystery of God.'
(Ashley and O'Rourke, *Health Care Ethics*, Catholic Hospital Association, St. Louis, Missouri. 1978)

> *See that you never despise*
> *any of these little ones,*
> *for I tell you*
> *that their angels in heaven*
> *are continually in the presence*
> *of my Father in heaven.*
>
> *(Mt 18:10)*

Their feast day is 28th December, the Feast of the Holy Innocents:

Herod was furious when he realised that he had been outwitted by the wise men, and in Bethlehem and its surrounding district he had all the male children killed who were two years old or under, reckoning by the date he had been careful to ask the wise men. It was then that the words spoken through the prophet Jeremiah were fulfilled:

A voice was heard in Ramah,
sobbing and loudly lamenting:
it was Rachel weeping for her children,
refusing to be comforted
because they were no more.(*Mt 2: 16-18*)

We do not doubt the salvation of these children.

God our Father,
you have called this child to yourself,
and already
he/she has entered eternal life.
Strengthen his/her parents
and relatives
in their sorrow.
May they find consolation
in knowing that,
in your infinite goodness,
you have taken him/her
into your loving care.
Amen.

(Christian Burial p 95)

Another most reassuring indication of God's purpose in this regard must be the doctrine of the Immaculate Conception, which declares that the Blessed Virgin Mary was without sin from the moment of her conception – without her being baptised, without a personal act of faith, without sharing in the faith of the Church, and without any sponsorship from the Christian community. Surely, this must be an indication of God's purpose and of the certainty of the salvation of all infants.

> *Lord God,*
> *Father of all consolation,*
> *May the father and mother (of this child)*
> *find comfort*
> *in knowing that you have taken him/her*
> *into your loving care.*
>
> *(Christian Burial p 103)*

'Nevertheless, it still is most important to administer baptism not so much because the child absolutely needs it, but in order to manifest the concern of the Church and thus to keep alive the consciousness of the dignity of the human person from the first moment of its existence. Consequently, nurses and doctors should baptise infants who are in danger of death and even miscarried fetuses which exhibit human form. They should pour water on the child (on the head, if possible) so as actually to touch the skin, and should say: "I baptise you in the name of the Father, and of the Son and of the Holy Spirit." In this way they have expressed Christian reverence and fellowship with this little person who will forever be part of the Trinitarian community.' (Ashley and O'Rourke, *Health Care Ethics*, Catholic Hospital Association, St Louis, Missouri, 1978.)

The Church never actually declared any teaching other than the above. No other teaching appears in the Scripture or in the writing of the early Fathers of the Church. Any other teaching clashes with the God revealed in Jesus Christ and with our sense of justice.

Your children ... in fact they are holy.

(1 Cor 7:14)
